Reflections On Resilience

Stories and Strategies for Thriving in Adversity

Elijah M. James, Ph. D.

Copyright © 2024 Elijah James
All rights reserved

No part of this book may be reproduced in any form or by any electronic or mechanical means without permission in writing from the author.

Canadian Cataloguing in Publication Data
James, Elijah M.
Reflections on Resilience: Stories and Strategies for Thriving in Adversity

ISBN 978-1-0690086-4-0

EJ Publishing
603 White Hills Run
Hammonds Plain
Nova Scotia, Canada B4B 1W7

To the loving memory of my parents, **Newton and Pearl**, who instilled in me the values of strength, perseverance, and grace. Through their unwavering example, I learned that resilience is not just about overcoming adversity but also about embracing life with courage, faith, and hope. Their love and wisdom continue to guide me each day, and this book is a tribute to the countless lessons they taught me about thriving in the face of challenges.

Reflections on Resilience
Table of Contents

Preface 1

Introduction 5
Overview of Resilience 5
Purpose of the Book 6
How to Use This Book 6

Part I Understanding Resilience 9

Chapter 1 The Core of Resilience 10
Introduction 10
What is Resilience? 10
The Science Behind Resilience 13
Why Resilience Matters Today 14
Conclusion 16
Further Reading 17

Chapter 2 Developing a Resilient Mindset 18
Introduction 18
What is Resilience? Exploring the Psychological and Emotional Foundation 18
The Growth Mindset vs. Fixed Mindset 19
Self-Compassion and Resilience 20
Strategies for Building Mental Toughness 22
Conclusion 23
Further Reading 23

Part II Stories of Resilience in Action 25

Chapter 3 Overcoming Physical Challenges.. 26

Introduction 26
Inspirational Stories of Physical Resilience 26
Strategies for Physical and Emotional Strength 29
Reflections on Body and Mind Resilience 31
Conclusion 31
Further Reading 31

Chapter 4 Resilience Through Emotional Hardships 32

Introduction 32
Stories of Emotional Recovery 33
Building Emotional Resilience 34
Reflection Exercise 37
Conclusion 37
Further Reading 38

Chapter 5 Professional Setbacks and Career Resilience 39

Introduction 39
Navigating Career Challenges 39
Strategies for Professional Growth During Hardship 42
Building a Support Network at Work 43
Professional Support and Career Resilience 45
Conclusion 45
Further Reading 46

Part III Strategies for Building Resilience in Daily Life 47

Chapter 6 Cultivating Resilience in Relationships 48

Introduction 48
Stories of Resilient Relationships: Overcoming Relational Conflicts and Losses 48

The Importance of Community and Support Systems: How to Create and Rely on Social Support 50
Communication Techniques for Difficult Times: Strengthening Connections Through Resilience 51
Conclusion 52
Further Reading 52

Chapter 7 Financial Resilience and Economic Adversity 53

Introduction 53
Personal Stories of Financial Recovery 53
Strategies for Financial Resilience 55
Learning Financial Literacy Skills 57
Conclusion 58
Further Reading 59

Chapter 8 Mental Health Resilience 60

Introduction 60
Navigating Mental Health Challenges 60
Building Daily Mental Health Habits 62
Reflection Exercise: Identifying Personal Coping Mechanisms and Support Networks 63
Conclusion 64
Further Reading 64

Part IV Thriving Beyond Adversity 65

Chapter 9 Transforming Failure into Growth 66

Introduction 66
Stories of Personal Transformation 67
Learning from Mistakes 68
Reflection Example: Turning Personal Failure into Growth 69
Conclusion 70
Further Reading 71

Chapter 10 Building Resilience Through Faith and Spirituality ... 72

Introduction ... 72
Stories of Spiritual Resilience ... 73
Spiritual Practices that Support Resilience ... 74
Reflection Exercises ... 76
The Interconnection of Mind, Body, and Spirit ... 77
Conclusion ... 77
Further Reading ... 78

Chapter 11 Using Creativity as a Resilience Tool ... 79

Introduction ... 79
Creative Expressions of Resilience ... 79
How Creativity Fosters Resilience ... 82
Finding Your Creative Outlet ... 83
Reflection Exercise ... 84
Conclusion ... 84
Further Reading ... 85

Chapter 12 Lifelong Learning and Adaptability ... 86

Introduction ... 86
Stories of Resilient Learners ... 87
The Role of Curiosity and Adaptability in Resilience ... 88
Building a Lifelong Learning Mindset ... 91
Reflection Exercise ... 92
Conclusion ... 93
Further Reading ... 93

Part V Moving Forward with Resilience ... 95

Chapter 13 Building a Resilient Community 96

Introduction ... 96
The Importance of Community ... 97

Collective Resilience Stories: How Communities Come Together During Adversity............................ 99
Strategies for Community Building and Support: Volunteering, Organizing, and Leading 101
Reflection Exercise: Assessing and Strengthening Local and Global Connections............................. 103
Conclusion... 104
Further Reading... 105

Chapter 14 Sustaining Resilience Over the Long Term 106

Introduction... 106
Real-life Stories.. 106
Resilience as a Lifelong Journey 108
Daily Practices for Maintaining Resilience........... 109
Setting Goals for Continued Growth 110
Conclusion... 111
Further Reading... 112

Conclusion: Reflecting on Your Resilience Journey.. 113

Summarizing Key Takeaways.............................. 113
Looking Forward with Hope and Determination .. 114
Encouraging Personal Reflection 115

Preface

Resilience is a concept that is often discussed in times of hardship, but it's much more than just a response to adversity. It's an ongoing journey—a skillset that enables us to overcome life's many challenges while continuing to grow and thrive. *Reflections on Resilience: Stories and Strategies for Thriving in Adversity* is the result of a deep desire to explore how ordinary people confront extraordinary challenges and, in doing so, emerge with renewed strength and wisdom. This book aims to shed light on resilience as a multi-faceted, life-sustaining force, one that goes beyond surviving hard times to actually thriving in the face of them.

The stories shared here represent the power of human determination, illustrating how diverse experiences—from personal loss to financial struggles and mental health challenges—can serve as powerful opportunities for growth. These stories are not just about bouncing back, but about the profound ways in which hardship can transform us. As we listen to the journeys of others, we see that resilience is not a trait reserved for a select few; it is within all of us, waiting to be nurtured.

At its core, this book explores resilience in its many forms: emotional, spiritual, financial, communal, and mental. Through a combination of real-life stories, practical strategies, and reflective exercises, it offers readers both inspiration and tools to cultivate resilience in their own lives. Whether it's through building daily habits that foster emotional strength, using creativity as a healing outlet, or finding comfort in community support, there are myriad ways to reinforce resilience.

As you read through these chapters, I encourage you to think deeply about your own life and the moments where resilience has played a role. Whether those moments were small or life-altering, they offer valuable lessons about who we are and how we face the world. This book aims to serve as both a guide and a companion for anyone seeking to build resilience over the long term, equipping you with the insights and inspiration to face future challenges with hope, courage, and determination.

Reflections on Resilience is a journey through the human spirit's capacity to endure, adapt, and thrive. I hope these stories and strategies will not only resonate with you but also empower you to strengthen your personal resilience, to face adversity with greater confidence, and to ultimately lead a more fulfilling life.

Acknowledgements

Writing *Reflections on Resilience* has been a deeply personal and inspiring journey, and I am immensely grateful to the many people who have supported and inspired me along the way.

PREFACE

First, my deepest thanks to my family, whose love and encouragement have been a constant source of strength. This book is a reflection of the lessons my late parents, Newton and Pearl, imparted, and I am forever indebted to them for their guidance.

To my close friends and colleagues, your unwavering support has been invaluable. You listened, shared wisdom, and reminded me of the power of community in difficult times. A special thanks to those who shared their stories of resilience with me. Your courage in adversity has been a source of deep inspiration for this work.

I also wish to express my gratitude to my caregivers and medical professionals, Dr. P. Matthews and Dr. Gerry Simon as well as Mr. Dane Batchelor and Mr. D. Simon whose compassion and expertise have played a vital role in my continued recovery and well-being. Koren, your love and care know no bounds.

Finally, to my readers: Thank you for allowing this book into your lives. My hope is that it serves as a reminder that, no matter the trials you face, resilience lies within you, ready to be cultivated and strengthened.

May this book be a source of hope, strength, and inspiration to all who encounter it.

REFLECTIONS ON RESILIENCE

Introduction

Overview of Resilience

Resilience is the ability to navigate through life's challenges with adaptability, courage, and persistence. It doesn't mean avoiding hardships but finding ways to move forward despite them, discovering strengths and strategies that allow us to thrive. In today's fast-paced world, where uncertainties in both personal and professional spheres are common, resilience has become more critical than ever. People encounter numerous challenges—ranging from economic hardships and health crises to personal losses and unexpected life changes. Building resilience equips us not only to handle immediate obstacles but also to grow through them, allowing us to shape our lives with a greater sense of purpose and stability.

As research in psychology, neuroscience, and social sciences has shown, resilience isn't a fixed trait. It's a set of skills, mindsets, and behaviorus that we can develop and strengthen over time. This book explores resilience through real stories and research-based strategies, offering readers pathways to grow in their ability to adapt and thrive, even in the face of adversity.

Purpose of the Book

The purpose of *Reflections on Resilience* is to provide inspiration and practical tools for people seeking to build resilience in their lives. By sharing stories of individuals who have faced diverse forms of adversity and emerged stronger, this book highlights the personal journeys that reveal resilience as a universal quality within each of us. These stories are accompanied by strategies that readers can apply to their own lives, creating a resource that combines both inspiration and actionable guidance.

Through this blend of narrative and practical advice, the book aims to support readers in understanding resilience on a personal level. It encourages self-reflection and provides tools to cultivate resilience as an ongoing, evolving journey. Whether you're navigating a difficult period or simply looking to strengthen your adaptability, this book is designed to support you in facing challenges with courage and clarity.

How to Use This Book

Reflections on Resilience is structured to allow readers to move through the material in a way that best supports their unique needs. Here are some ways to engage with the book for maximum benefit:

Personal Reflections

Each chapter includes questions and prompts to help readers reflect on their own experiences, values, and goals. These can be used as journal prompts or discussed with friends, family, or support groups.

Resilience Exercises

Practical exercises, found throughout the chapters, offer techniques for building resilience skills, such as mindfulness practices, stress management strategies, and goal-setting exercises. These are intended to be hands-on and adaptable, suitable for readers at any stage of their resilience journey.

Story-Based Inspiration

Stories throughout the book provide a variety of perspectives on resilience, showing that challenges can be transformative. Readers can turn to these stories for motivation, understanding, and empathy, as they reveal both the universality of struggle and the individual nature of resilience.

Whether you're reading cover to cover or focusing on particular sections, this book is designed to be a supportive companion in strengthening your resilience and enriching your life journey.

REFLECTIONS ON RESILIENCE

Part I
Understanding Resilience

Chapter 1
The Core of Resilience

Introduction

In today's dynamic and often turbulent world, the ability to adapt and flourish amidst hardship is crucial. Resilience, a trait often associated with emotional strength and mental toughness, has taken on new dimensions in the modern context. Beyond simply "bouncing back," resilience embodies a mindset that embraces adversity, using it as fuel for growth. In this chapter, we'll explore resilience's psychological and biological foundations and examine why this skill is critical now more than ever. By delving into the science and rationale behind resilience, we aim to equip readers with a solid understanding of this vital attribute, setting the stage for deeper, practical exploration throughout this book.

What is Resilience?

At its core, resilience is more than just overcoming obstacles—it is a process of positive adaptation. Researchers define resilience as the capacity to withstand and recover from difficulties, but it also involves transforming challenges into opportunities for self-improvement. Psychologists often describe resilience as a blend of emotional regulation, cognitive flexibility, and a growth-oriented mindset.

According to the American Psychological Association:

Resilience is the process and outcome of successfully adapting to difficult or challenging life experiences, especially through mental, emotional, and behavioral flexibility and adjustment to external and internal demands.

https://www.apa.org/topics/resilience

A key aspect of resilience is cognitive reframing, the ability to shift perspective and see setbacks as learning experiences. This is not merely "positive thinking" but a deliberate approach to reinterpreting adversities constructively. For example, resilient people often assess past difficulties to find lessons, which reinforces self-efficacy—the belief in one's capability to manage future challenges.

According to Dr. Ann Masten, a leading researcher in resilience, this quality can be compared to "ordinary magic" because it is a natural but powerful process available to everyone. Masten's research, especially her work on child resilience, shows that even children in severe poverty or with significant trauma can thrive when given proper support systems, a point that highlights resilience's inherent and often untapped potential in all of us.

Examples of Resilient People
Elizabeth Smart: Overcoming Trauma

In 2002, Elizabeth Smart was abducted from her home at the age of 14 and held captive for nine months by a man and his wife who subjected her to unimaginable abuse. Despite the trauma, Elizabeth demonstrated remarkable resilience after her rescue. Rather than allowing the experience to define her, she became an advocate for missing children and survivors of sexual violence. Her ability to rebuild her life and use her platform for positive change is a testament to the strength of the human spirit. Smart's story reminds us that resilience is not just about surviving adversity but transforming it into a force for good.

Stephen Hawking: Thriving with ALS

When world-renowned physicist Stephen Hawking was diagnosed with ALS (Amyotrophic Lateral Sclerosis) at the age of 21, doctors gave him only a few years to live. Despite his debilitating condition, which gradually left him almost completely paralyzed, Hawking went on to revolutionize our understanding of black holes and the universe. His resilience allowed him to adapt, relying on assistive technology to continue his groundbreaking work. Hawking's unwavering determination in the face of physical limitations demonstrates how mental and emotional resilience can help us overcome even the most severe challenges.

The Science Behind Resilience

Advances in neuroscience have significantly expanded our understanding of resilience. Resilience isn't solely a personality trait but is deeply embedded in biological processes. The following are core findings from recent studies in this area:

Brain Structures

The prefrontal cortex (PFC) plays a pivotal role in regulating emotions and managing stress. This area of the brain aids in decision-making, impulse control, and interpreting stressful events with a broader perspective. In resilient individuals, the PFC communicates effectively with the amygdala, the brain's emotional center responsible for processing fear and stress responses. Together, they create a balanced reaction, preventing overreactions to stress.

Neuroplasticity

Resilience is also a product of neuroplasticity, the brain's ability to form new neural pathways. Positive coping strategies, like mindfulness or reinterpreting negative events, can help "rewire" the brain, enhancing resilience. For instance, repeated practice of reframing setbacks as growth opportunities strengthens connections in the brain associated with resilience, making individuals better equipped to face future adversity.

Genetic and Environmental Influences

Genetic studies reveal that some people may be naturally more predisposed to resilience owing to variations in genes related to stress response. However, environment and learned behaviours are equally powerful. Supportive social relationships, meaningful life roles, and effective coping mechanisms can significantly influence resilience. Studies on people who have overcome trauma demonstrate that external support networks, such as family or community, often play a defining role in fostering resilience, reinforcing the idea that resilience is both an individual and collective endeavour.

Why Resilience Matters Today

In an era defined by rapid technological advancements, economic shifts, and global crises such as pandemics, resilience has become an essential skill. Not only does resilience help individuals cope with everyday stress, but it also enables society to collectively manage larger-scale adversities. The importance of resilience in today's world can be observed in three significant areas:

Adaptation to Change

As we face constant changes in work environments, social dynamics, and even environmental conditions, resilience serves as a mental "stabilizer." It helps people accept change as an inevitable part of life, encouraging proactive adjustment rather than passive endurance. For instance, in the workplace, resilient employees are more likely to embrace organizational changes, contributing to smoother transitions and a healthier work culture.

Mental Health and Well-being

Resilience directly impacts mental health, providing a buffer against anxiety, depression, and burnout. Research indicates that resilient individuals are more adept at handling stress without succumbing to negative mental health outcomes. By reinforcing emotional and psychological defenses, resilience promotes a state of well-being even amid stressful circumstances, allowing individuals to enjoy a sense of purpose and satisfaction.

Fostering Collective Strength

On a societal level, resilience supports collective strength in communities. During natural disasters, economic recessions, or social upheavals, resilient communities demonstrate solidarity, supporting one another to rebuild. For example, studies on post-trauma communities show that social resilience—collective adaptability and mutual support—leads to faster recovery and greater long-term stability.

Practical Tips for Building Resilience

Building resilience is an ongoing process that requires intentional practice. Here are several strategies that research has shown to effectively cultivate resilience:

Mindfulness and Meditation

Practicing mindfulness can help individuals become more present and less reactive to stressors, encouraging a calm, measured response to challenges. Regular meditation has been shown to alter the brain's structure, enhancing areas responsible for emotional regulation.

Fostering Connections

Strong social networks can act as a "safety net" during tough times. Developing close relationships with family, friends, or support groups provides emotional support and practical guidance, increasing resilience in the face of adversity.

Setting Realistic Goals

Goal-setting helps people to focus on manageable steps rather than becoming overwhelmed by the magnitude of a challenge. Resilient individuals often break down their objectives, reinforcing a sense of progress and achievement.

Developing Emotional Regulation Skills

Emotions are integral to resilience, and managing them effectively is crucial. Techniques such as journaling or practicing gratitude can help individuals process their emotions constructively, preventing them from feeling overwhelmed.

Regular Physical Exercise

Physical health supports mental resilience. Exercise has been shown to reduce stress, improve mood, and enhance cognitive function, all of which contribute to resilience.

Conclusion

Resilience stands as a foundational skill for thriving in modern life, enabling individuals and communities to withstand and grow through adversity. Understanding resilience's psychological and neurological roots, its relevance in today's unpredictable world, and practical ways to cultivate it empowers us to face challenges with optimism and strength. As we journey through this book, remember that resilience is not a fixed trait but a capacity we all possess and can develop over time. Embracing resilience allows us to lead more fulfilling, purposeful lives despite life's uncertainties.

Further Reading

Masten, Ann S. *Ordinary Magic: Resilience in Development.* Guilford Press, 2014.

Southwick, Steven M., and Dennis S. Charney, *Resilience: The Science of Mastering Life's Greatest Challenges.* Cambridge University Press, 2018.

Chapter 2
Developing a Resilient Mindset

Introduction

Building resilience is a journey rooted in the development of healthy mental habits and strong emotional foundations. In an increasingly unpredictable world, a resilient mindset allows individuals to face setbacks and thrive despite adversity. This chapter explores the essential mindsets, such as growth and self-compassion, as well as practical methods for building resilience. With each section, you'll find real-life examples, step-by-step exercises, and reflection prompts to help you apply these principles and develop a mindset prepared for any challenges that lie ahead.

What is Resilience? Exploring the Psychological and Emotional Foundation

Resilience is more than merely bouncing back; it's about adapting, learning, and sometimes even thriving in the face of hardship. At its core, resilience is grounded in an attitude that setbacks are temporary and surmountable. Psychologists emphasize that resilience isn't a fixed trait but rather a skill that can be cultivated through effort and intentional mental strategies.

Real-Life Example

Jane, a corporate manager, faced the challenge of restructuring her team after unexpected layoffs. Instead of succumbing to the pressure, she reframed the situation, asking herself, "How can this change improve our team's performance?" By focusing on potential opportunities, Jane not only coped with the restructuring but also helped her team become more cohesive and productive.

Reflection Prompt

Think of a recent setback. How might reframing it as an opportunity for growth change your perspective?

The Growth Mindset vs. Fixed Mindset

A growth mindset—the belief that abilities can be developed—is foundational for resilience. Unlike a fixed mindset, where people view challenges as threats to their abilities, a growth mindset enables individuals to see challenges as opportunities to learn and grow. Psychologist Carol Dweck, who pioneered the concept, explains that growth-oriented individuals are more likely to persevere, adapt, and emerge stronger from adversity.

Real-Life Example: Thomas Edison

Thomas Edison famously endured thousands of failed experiments before inventing the light bulb. Rather than viewing each failure as a permanent defeat, he saw it as one more step toward success. His growth mindset enabled him to innovate and thrive despite repeated setbacks, exemplifying resilience in action.

Practical Exercise:
Growth Mindset Journaling

To develop a growth mindset, take five minutes at the end of each day to reflect on challenges you encountered:

1. Identify one challenge and describe how you initially responded to it.
2. Ask yourself: "What did I learn from this experience? How can I improve next time?"
3. Write down one positive action you can take in future, similar situations.

Reflection Prompts

1. Are there specific areas in your life where you view challenges as permanent limitations?
2. How can adopting a growth mindset help you approach these challenges with renewed optimism?

Self-Compassion and Resilience

Self-compassion, according to researcher Kristin Neff, is a critical yet often overlooked component of resilience. When faced with setbacks, self-compassion allows us to recognize our common humanity, forgive our mistakes, and approach future challenges with a balanced perspective. This acceptance of imperfection leads to greater persistence and resilience over time.

Real-Life Example: Kristin Neff's Journey in Self-Compassion

During her Ph.D., Neff faced severe self-doubt and perfectionism. By practicing self-compassion, she was able to move beyond self-criticism and complete her program. This experience led her to pioneer research on self-compassion's role in mental resilience.

Practical Exercise: Self-Compassion Break

When you encounter a difficult situation, take three mindful breaths and repeat these three steps:

1. **Acknowledge the hardship:** "This is really tough for me."
2. **Offer kindness:** "I'm doing my best, and I'll be patient with myself."
3. **Commit to growth:** "I will use this as an opportunity to learn and grow."

Reflection Prompts

1. In moments of difficulty, do you tend to judge yourself harshly?
2. How could practicing self-compassion make you more resilient?

Strategies for Building Mental Toughness

Mental toughness helps you endure stress with calm and clarity. It's the ability to stay focused on long-term goals and maintain optimism, even in the face of setbacks.

Real-Life Example: Michael Jordan's Resilience

Cut from his high school basketball team, Michael Jordan could have given up on his dream. Instead, he viewed the setback as motivation, ultimately becoming one of the most accomplished players in NBA history. His mental toughness fueled his resilience, allowing him to pursue his goals despite early failure.

Practical Exercise: Visualization for Mental Toughness

1. Find a quiet space and close your eyes. Picture a challenging situation.
2. Visualize yourself handling the situation with confidence, clarity, and calm.
3. Imagine the satisfaction of overcoming the challenge and achieving your goals.

Practicing visualization regularly can prepare your mind to respond to real challenges with resilience.

Reflection Prompts

1. What challenging situations cause you anxiety?
2. How might visualizing successful outcomes help you feel more prepared?

Conclusion

Developing a resilient mindset is a journey that requires practice, patience, and self-compassion. By embracing a growth mindset, showing yourself kindness, and building mental toughness, you can cultivate resilience to face life's inevitable challenges with strength and determination. Each step forward, however small, contributes to a more resilient mindset and a more fulfilling life.

Further Reading

Dweck, Carol. *Mindset: The New Psychology of Success.* Ballantine Books, 2006.

Jordan, Michael, and Mark Vancil. *For the Love of the Game: My Story.* Crown Publishers, 1998.

Siebert, Al. *The Resiliency Advantage: Master Change, Thrive Under Pressure, and Bounce Back from Setbacks.* Berrett-Koehler Publishers, 2005.

REFLECTIONS ON RESILIENCE

Part II
Stories of Resilience in Action

Chapter 3
Overcoming Physical Challenges

Introduction

Physical challenges often test the limits of human resilience. For many, facing a sudden injury, illness, or a chronic condition can be daunting, reshaping daily life and personal identity. Beyond the physical adjustments, individuals must often contend with emotional, psychological, and social hurdles, as these challenges can affect self-worth, relationships, and professional ambitions. Yet, it is through these adversities that the human spirit can emerge even stronger. In this chapter, we explore inspiring stories of resilience and provide strategies to cultivate physical and mental strength in the face of physical challenges.

Inspirational Stories of Physical Resilience

Real-life experiences often demonstrate resilience in ways that theory cannot. Here, we delve into the stories of those who have found strength in adversity, providing lessons on the importance of adaptability, perseverance, and self-discovery.

John's Marathon Comeback

John, an avid marathon runner, suffered a devastating spinal injury in a car accident. Initially paralyzed from the waist down, he was informed that running again might not be possible. For John, running had been a part of his identity and a source of joy and release. The prospect of losing it was emotionally crushing. However, he focused on what he could control: his mindset.

Strategies He Used

1. **Setting Micro-Goals:** John focused on achieving tiny goals—first, moving a toe, then strengthening his core.
2. **Embracing Rehabilitation:** Despite grueling days of physical therapy, John committed himself to every session with a positive attitude. His incremental goals eventually led to jogging and, two years later, a triumphant return to the marathon circuit.

Reflection Prompt

Have you ever faced a physical or emotional setback that challenged your identity? How did you find ways to adapt and redefine yourself?

Emily's Journey with Chronic Pain

Diagnosed with fibromyalgia, Emily endured chronic pain that affected her ability to work and socialize. Daily tasks became monumental, and she grappled with feelings of isolation. While pain management strategies helped, Emily realized that acceptance and mental fortitude were equally vital in her journey.

Strategies She Used

1. **Building a Support System:** Emily joined an online support group that provided her with community, validation, and shared resources for pain management.
2. **Practicing Mindfulness:** Emily began practicing mindfulness to manage her pain better, focusing on mental clarity and emotional acceptance rather than physical limitations.

Reflection Prompt

How do you respond when facing a problem that has no clear solution? What sources of support do you seek out?

Adapting to Change After Limb Loss

For Rachel, a professional artist, losing her dominant arm in a workplace accident led to a loss of identity as she could no longer paint as she once did. Rachel's resilience came from her determination to adapt: she started painting with her left hand and eventually learned to use digital tools, opening a new dimension to her art.

Strategies She Used

1. **Exploring Alternative Methods:** Rachel adapted by learning to create with her non-dominant hand and embracing digital media.

2. **Finding New Inspiration:** By exploring new art forms, Rachel rediscovered joy and passion for her work, fostering resilience through creative adaptation.

Reflection Prompt

Consider a skill or activity you enjoy. How would you adapt if circumstances forced you to approach it differently?

Strategies for Physical and Emotional Strength

Building resilience involves more than physical recovery; it requires developing mental and emotional strength. Here are core strategies to help individuals facing physical challenges:

1. Setting Incremental Goals

Recovery can be overwhelming, and incremental goals allow individuals to focus on manageable steps. Goals such as improving flexibility or increasing endurance can offer concrete achievements that build momentum.

Exercise: Setting SMART Goals

Write down a long-term goal related to physical or emotional resilience. Break it down into smaller, Specific, Measurable, Achievable, Relevant, and Time-bound (SMART) goals to track progress.

2. Seeking and Building Support Systems

Whether family, friends, or support groups, surrounding oneself with positive reinforcement is critical. Support networks provide encouragement, share coping strategies, and offer emotional solace.

Exercise: Mapping Your Support Network

List individuals or groups who support you in different areas of your life (emotional, physical, or practical). Consider reaching out to them and exploring how they can assist you in building resilience.

3. Cultivating a Mind-Body Connection

Practices like yoga, mindfulness, and deep breathing exercises connect the mind and body, helping individuals manage stress and approach physical challenges with a clearer mindset.

Reflection Prompt

How often do you take time to relax and reconnect with your body? Consider exploring practices that help you feel more at ease in your physical self.

4. Accepting and Celebrating Small Victories

Recovery is often nonlinear. Celebrating progress fosters resilience by emphasizing how far one has come, encouraging individuals to keep pushing forward despite setbacks.

Reflection Exercise: Daily Achievement Journal

Write down one achievement each day, no matter how small. This habit reinforces self-worth and builds resilience over time.

Reflections on Body and Mind Resilience

Physical challenges often serve as tests of mental fortitude, requiring individuals to harness emotional resilience to cope with the physical limitations they face. Embracing both the limitations and the strengths of one's body can provide a balanced outlook on resilience.

Mindfulness Reflection Exercise

Spend a few minutes each day observing and accepting any physical discomfort without judgment. Reflect on your reactions, and allow yourself to accept and manage the sensations calmly. This exercise fosters resilience by building mental endurance and acceptance.

Conclusion

Physical resilience involves far more than the body alone. It encompasses the mind, emotions, and spirit. Those who face physical adversity develop new perspectives, harness inner strength, and emerge with a profound understanding of their own resilience. As individuals work to overcome their physical challenges, they come to understand that resilience is not only about recovery but about growth, adaptation, and embracing life in all its forms.

Further Reading

Kabat-Zinn, Jon. *Full Catastrophe Living: Using the Wisdom of Your Body and Mind to Face Stress, Pain, and Illness.* Bantam, 2013.

Seligman, Martin E.P. *The Hope Circuit: A Psychologist's Journey from Helplessness to Optimism.* Hachette Books, 2018.

Chapter 4
Resilience Through Emotional Hardships

Introduction

Emotional hardships are inevitable in life, touching everyone at some point. These hardships, whether stemming from loss, trauma, failed relationships, or chronic stress, have the potential to profoundly affect one's emotional well-being. However, just as individuals face emotional turmoil, they also have the ability to overcome and grow stronger from these experiences. Emotional resilience is the strength that allows us to endure and thrive in the face of adversity, transforming hardships into opportunities for personal growth.

In this chapter, we will explore the concept of emotional resilience through real-life stories, discuss practical strategies to develop this strength, and offer reflection exercises to help you navigate your emotional challenges. Whether you're dealing with grief, anxiety, or emotional exhaustion, this chapter will equip you with tools to build emotional fortitude and emerge stronger.

Stories of Emotional Recovery

Real-life stories often demonstrate the incredible potential of the human spirit to endure emotional turmoil and come out stronger. Here are some inspiring examples of individuals who have built emotional resilience after significant challenges:

Sarah's Journey of Grief to Purpose

Sarah lost her husband in a tragic car accident. In the months following his death, she fell into a deep depression, feeling paralyzed by grief. The pain of his loss consumed her every thought. Yet, despite this overwhelming sorrow, she realized that her husband would have wanted her to live fully. Gradually, Sarah began seeking support, attending grief counseling, and sharing her experiences with others in similar situations. Over time, she found purpose in helping others navigate their own losses. Today, Sarah works as a grief counselor, and through her resilience, she has transformed her pain into a source of strength for herself and others.

David's Triumph Over Anxiety

David, a successful lawyer, battled severe anxiety for much of his professional career. The pressures of his job, combined with his personal perfectionism, created a cycle of self-doubt and mental exhaustion. After a particularly difficult case, David reached a breaking point and sought therapy. Through cognitive-behavioural therapy

(CBT), mindfulness meditation, and gradually confronting his fears, he developed emotional resilience. David now uses his story to mentor others in high-pressure jobs, showing them that overcoming anxiety is possible through patience, self-care, and persistence.

Maria's Resilience Amid Financial Hardships

Maria was a single mother who faced extreme financial hardship after losing her job. The stress of providing for her children while dealing with her personal emotional turmoil was overwhelming. However, Maria leaned into her network of friends and community resources, seeking emotional support and financial advice. She started by setting small goals, keeping herself emotionally grounded despite the uncertainty. Over time, Maria secured a new job and became an advocate for single mothers, helping them handle the emotional challenges that come with financial instability.

These stories reveal that emotional resilience is not about eliminating hardship but about finding strength in adversity. These individuals faced profound emotional pain but used their experiences as stepping stones for growth, healing, and purpose.

Building Emotional Resilience

Building emotional resilience is a process that requires intentional effort and self-awareness. Here are key strategies to help develop and maintain emotional resilience:

Acknowledge and Accept Emotions

The first step in building emotional resilience is to acknowledge and accept your feelings rather than suppress them. Emotions such as sadness, anger, or frustration are normal reactions to hardship, and suppressing them can prolong emotional distress. Mindfulness practices, such as journaling or meditation, allow you to process emotions in a healthy way, giving you the emotional space to reflect and respond rather than react.

Develop a Strong Support System

Emotional resilience is not cultivated in isolation. Surrounding yourself with supportive individuals, whether family, friends, or a professional counselor, is crucial. These relationships provide comfort during difficult times and allow you to share your struggles without judgment. Building connections with others who can listen, empathize, and offer support strengthens your emotional well-being.

Practice Self-Compassion

Self-compassion is essential for resilience. Instead of being critical of yourself when facing hardships, practicing kindness and understanding towards yourself allows you to move through difficult times without adding self-imposed emotional burden. Dr. Kristin Neff's research on self-compassion shows that those who are kind to themselves during adversity are more likely to bounce back from emotional hardships. Self-compassion practices include speaking kindly to yourself, accepting your flaws, and taking time for self-care.

Learn Emotional Regulation Techniques

Emotional regulation is the ability to manage and respond to emotions effectively, especially during challenging situations. Techniques such as deep breathing, progressive muscle relaxation, and mindfulness meditation can help you stay calm and focused during emotional upheavals. Emotional regulation is a cornerstone of resilience because it helps you avoid impulsive reactions and fosters thoughtful, grounded responses to stress.

Challenge Negative Thought Patterns

Cognitive-behavioural therapy (CBT) techniques can help challenge negative or irrational thought patterns that often accompany emotional distress. By learning to recognize distorted thinking—such as catastrophizing or black-and-white thinking—you can begin to reframe these thoughts in a more positive and realistic light. For example, instead of thinking, "I'll never get through this," you can reframe it as, "This is difficult, but I have the strength to overcome it."

Find Meaning in Hardship

Resilience is often about finding meaning or purpose in emotional hardship. Viktor Frankl, a psychiatrist and Holocaust survivor, emphasized the power of finding meaning in suffering. When you're able to view hardship as an opportunity for growth or a learning experience, it can make emotional pain more bearable. Reflecting on the lessons that come from adversity allows you to integrate those experiences into a more resilient mindset.

Reflection Exercise

Building Emotional Resilience Through Reflection

Identify an Emotional Hardship: Reflect on a recent emotional challenge. Write down the situation and the emotions you experienced.

What Did You Learn?: Think about how you responded to the situation. What did you learn about yourself? Did you react with resilience, or did you struggle to cope?

Applying Resilience Strategies: Choose one of the resilience-building strategies discussed in this chapter—whether it's mindfulness, self-compassion, or emotional regulation—and apply it to the emotional hardship you identified. Write down how using this strategy might have helped you handle the situation differently.

Future Application: How can you apply what you've learned to future emotional challenges? Reflect on how these resilience strategies can become part of your regular emotional practice.

Conclusion

Building emotional resilience is a lifelong process, but the rewards are profound. By acknowledging and accepting your emotions, cultivating strong support systems, and practicing emotional regulation, you can overcome even the most difficult emotional hardships. Resilience doesn't mean avoiding pain but learning to grow and thrive despite it. With the strategies and reflection exercises in this chapter, you can begin to build your emotional resilience and emerge from adversity stronger and more capable.

Further Reading

Brown, Brené. *Rising Strong: How the Ability to Reset Transforms the Way We Live, Love, Parent, and Lead.* Spiegel & Grau, 2015.

David, Susan. *Emotional Agility: Get Unstuck, Embrace Change, and Thrive in Work and Life.* Penguin Books, 2016.

Sandberg, Sheryl, and Adam Grant. *Option B: Facing Adversity, Building Resilience, and Finding Joy.* Knopf, 2017.

Chapter 5
Professional Setbacks and Career Resilience

Introduction
Dealing with professional setbacks is an inevitable part of any career journey. Whether it's facing a missed promotion, dealing with job loss, or enduring conflicts in the workplace, challenges in the professional sphere can deeply affect not only your career but also your sense of identity and well-being. Building resilience is essential to bouncing back from these obstacles and finding growth through adversity. This chapter explores how to handle career challenges, grow professionally in difficult times, and develop a robust support network to thrive in the workplace.

Navigating Career Challenges
Professional setbacks can take many forms. Whether you're dealing with an uncooperative manager, being overlooked for a raise or promotion, or grappling with a career change,

coping with these situations with resilience is essential. The following individuals have shown resilience in their careers.

Steve Jobs and the Creation of Apple (Resilience After Being Fired)

After co-founding *Apple* and reaching global success, *Steve Jobs* was famously ousted from the company he had helped create because of a dramatic board dispute. However, rather than accepting defeat, Jobs embraced his professional setback as an opportunity to create new ventures. He founded *NeXT*, which paved the way for the development of the innovative technology that ultimately led to the rebirth of Apple. Through the 1990s, he acquired *Pixar*, which became the revolutionary animation studio. His career comeback culminated when Apple acquired *NeXT*, and Jobs returned to lead Apple to unprecedented growth—turning *Apple* into the global icon it is today. This highlights the importance of resilience "setbacks" as key to long-term global success.

Vera Wang *and Late-Career Success*

Vera Wang, now a world-renowned fashion designer, faced a major professional setback early in her career. Originally an aspiring Olympic figure skater, Wang had to give up her skating career in her late teens after not making the U.S. Olympic team. She then transitioned into journalism, spending years as an editor at *Vogue*. However, she was passed over for the editor-in-chief role, a disappointment that led her to leave the magazine. At age 40, she embarked on a new career in fashion design, launching a bridal gown collection. Despite facing age-related challenges in an industry favouring younger designers, Wang's resilience and determination to reinvent herself resulted in an iconic global brand. Her journey underscores that professional setbacks can be the foundation for future success.

Reframe Setbacks as Opportunities for Growth

Rather than viewing career challenges as personal failures, consider them opportunities for growth. Reframing adversity helps you adopt a more constructive mindset that focuses on learning, adaptation, and future success. When facing a career setback, it's helpful to ask, "What can I learn from this?" instead of "Why did this happen to me?" By shifting your focus to personal and professional growth, you allow yourself to turn challenges into stepping stones for future success.

Reflection Prompt: Think about a time when you encountered a career setback. How did you react, and what lessons can you draw from that experience to apply in the future?

Flexibility and Adaptability

In an ever-changing professional landscape, flexibility is a critical skill. Being adaptable in the face of organizational changes, shifting roles, or technological advances can help you maintain resilience and continue growing. Professionals who embrace change and are willing to adjust their goals and strategies tend to bounce back faster from setbacks.

Exercise: Identify an area of your career where you've had to be flexible. How did that flexibility help you navigate a challenge? Write down ways you can cultivate more adaptability in your work life.

Strategies for Professional Growth During Hardship

Lifelong Learning and Skill Building

In moments of career stagnation or difficulty, investing in continuous learning can be one of the most effective ways to build resilience. Learning new skills—whether through formal education, online courses, or hands-on experience—not only keeps you competitive in the job market but also boosts your confidence and adaptability.

Real-Life Example: During the 2008 economic crisis, many professionals used the downturn as an opportunity to pursue further education, upskill, or even transition to entirely new industries. Their decision to invest in their own development during hardship opened up new career opportunities when the economy recovered.

Exercise: Set a goal to learn a new skill relevant to your industry over the next six months. Enroll in an online course, attend a workshop, or seek mentorship from a colleague to enhance your expertise.

Building Emotional Agility

Resilience in the workplace requires not only practical strategies but also emotional intelligence.

Emotional agility allows you to manage stress, process negative emotions, and make thoughtful decisions in difficult moments. By developing emotional awareness and practicing self-regulation, you can prevent setbacks from overwhelming you.

Reflection Prompt: Think about a recent stressful situation at work. How did you react emotionally? What can you do differently next time to manage your emotions more effectively?

Building a Support Network at Work

Professional support is a crucial pillar in fostering resilience. Whether it's through formal mentorship programs, peer relationships, or leadership support, a strong network can be an invaluable resource when dealing with career setbacks.

Mentorship and Sponsorship

Having a mentor or sponsor who can provide guidance and feedback is critical in handling career challenges. A mentor can offer insights into overcoming setbacks, and a sponsor can advocate for you in crucial moments. Both can play a vital role in helping you develop the resilience needed to persevere and succeed professionally.

Practical Tip: If you don't already have a mentor, consider reaching out to someone whose career path or leadership style you admire. Approach him/her with specific questions or challenges, and request periodic meetings for advice and mentorship.

Peer Support and Networking

In addition to having mentors, building strong peer relationships at work can also bolster resilience. Engaging with colleagues who understand the pressures of your industry or position can provide much-needed emotional support during difficult times. Peer support networks can offer fresh perspectives, practical solutions, and even opportunities for collaboration and innovation in your career.

Exercise: Identify colleagues or professional networks within your field where you can cultivate supportive, constructive relationships. Schedule regular meetups, whether formal or informal, to exchange ideas and share challenges.

Leadership and Organizational Support

Organizations play a key role in fostering employee resilience. A workplace culture that encourages open communication, collaboration, and mental well-being provides a solid foundation for individuals to overcome setbacks and bounce back from failure. Leaders should be proactive in recognizing the emotional and professional needs of their teams, ensuring they feel supported during times of stress or change.

Reflection Prompt: How would you assess your current work environment in terms of emotional and professional support? What changes could you make to foster more supportive relationships at work, whether in a leadership role or as a colleague?

Professional Support and Career Resilience

Building a professional support system doesn't stop at mentors and peers. It also extends to creating connections with a broader community. Professional associations, industry groups, and even online networks offer resources, advice, and opportunities to learn from others who have faced similar challenges. Resilient professionals often lean on these networks not just for emotional support but also for new career prospects and advice during transitions.

Practical Tip: Consider joining a professional organization within your industry or attending networking events, whether in person or virtual. These spaces can offer valuable resources, opportunities for learning, and emotional support when dealing with career challenges.

Conclusion

Professional setbacks are a natural part of any career, but building resilience allows you to grow through these experiences and emerge stronger. By cultivating a growth mindset, seeking continuous learning, building emotional agility, and leveraging professional support networks, you can cope with challenges with confidence and develop a more fulfilling career.

With the right strategies in place—whether it's embracing flexibility, seeking mentorship, or investing in your own learning—you can turn professional obstacles into opportunities for growth. Resilience is not about avoiding difficulty, but about learning to thrive in the face of it.

Further Reading

Dweck, Carol. *Mindset: The New Psychology of Success.* Random House, 2006.

Heath, Chip, and Dan Heath. *Switch: How to Change Things When Change Is Hard.* Crown Business, 2010.

Sandberg, Sheryl. *Option B: Facing Adversity, Building Resilience, and Finding Joy.* Knopf, 2017.

Part III
Strategies for Building Resilience in Daily Life

Chapter 6
Cultivating Resilience in Relationships

Introduction

Relationships are foundational to our well-being, providing support, love, and connection. However, every relationship, whether familial, romantic, or friendship-based, faces challenges. Resilience in relationships isn't just about weathering these storms but growing stronger through them. This chapter will explore how resilient relationships are formed and maintained, how conflicts are managed, and the importance of communication during difficult times.

Stories of Resilient Relationships: Overcoming Relational Conflicts and Losses

Many people face relational difficulties at some point—whether it's due to misunderstandings, life changes, or external stressors. A resilient relationship is one that adapts, learns, and moves forward despite adversity. Let's consider a few stories of individuals who have shown resilience in their relationships. Let us begin with John and Sarah.

Strengthening Marriage After Job Loss

John and Sarah had been married for over ten years when John unexpectedly lost his job. The financial strain put enormous pressure on their relationship, leading to frequent arguments. At one point, they considered separation. However, they sought counseling, where they learned to communicate more openly and understand each other's stress and fears. Over time, their relationship became stronger as they learned to support one another emotionally, becoming more resilient to future challenges.

Rebuilding Friendship After Betrayal

After a misunderstanding led to a falling out, two close friends, Maura and Laura, went years without speaking. However, through mutual friends and personal growth, they found their way back to one another. By acknowledging their mistakes, forgiving each other, and slowly rebuilding trust, they not only restored their friendship but deepened it.

These stories illustrate how setbacks can either weaken or strengthen relationships, depending on how they are handled. The key to overcoming conflict is often forgiveness, patience, and the willingness to communicate effectively.

The Importance of Community and Support Systems: How to Create and Rely on Social Support

No one is meant to face life's challenges alone. Social support systems—whether from friends, family, or community—play an integral role in resilience. Research shows that individuals with strong social networks are better equipped to manage stress and bounce back from hardship.

Building these support systems doesn't happen overnight. It takes time and effort to cultivate meaningful relationships. Here are some steps to help build and maintain a supportive community:

Be intentional in maintaining connections: Regularly check in on friends and family, even when life gets busy.

Invest in reciprocal relationships: Support should be a two-way street. Offer help to those in your network, and be willing to ask for help when needed.

Seek out communities of shared interests or values: Whether through religious organizations, clubs, or interest groups, being part of a community with shared beliefs or goals provides a sense of belonging and collective resilience.

Reflection Prompt: Think of a time when someone in your support system helped you through a difficult situation. How did that support impact your ability to cope? In what ways can you strengthen or expand your current support network?

Communication Techniques for Difficult Times: Strengthening Connections Through Resilience

Communication is essential in any relationship but becomes even more crucial during tough times. In moments of stress or conflict, miscommunication often exacerbates problems, creating unnecessary friction. Developing healthy communication techniques can help maintain trust and closeness in relationships, even when the going gets tough.

Here are a few strategies to consider:

Active Listening: Many conflicts arise from misunderstandings. Instead of focusing on how to respond, take the time to fully listen to the other person's perspective. This fosters empathy and helps to de-escalate tension.

Use "I" Statements: When addressing a problem, focus on how the situation makes *you* feel, rather than blaming the other person. For example, instead of saying "You never listen to me," try "I feel unheard when I share my concerns."

Timing Matters: Difficult conversations should not happen in the heat of the moment. Wait until both parties are calm and able to discuss the issue without heightened emotions.

Stay Open to Compromise: Resilient relationships are about give and take. Be open to finding a middle ground and compromising when necessary to maintain the health of the relationship.

Exercise

The next time you face a challenging conversation, practice using "I" statements to express your emotions. Afterward, reflect on how this communication method impacted the conversation. Did it lead to better understanding and resolution?

Conclusion

Resilient relationships are not free from conflict or hardship. In fact, it is through adversity that many relationships are strengthened. By learning from setbacks, investing in strong social networks, and developing effective communication techniques, individuals can build relationships that endure through life's ups and downs.

Further Reading

Brown, Brené. *The Power of Vulnerability: Teachings on Authenticity, Connection, and Courage.* Sounds True, 2013.

Johnson, Sue. *Hold Me Tight: Seven Conversations for a Lifetime of Love.* Little, Brown and Company, 2008.

Chapter 7
Financial Resilience and Economic Adversity

Introduction

Financial hardship is a reality that many people face at some point in their lives, whether owing to job loss, medical expenses, debt, or global economic downturns. While financial challenges can be overwhelming, the ability to develop resilience in these circumstances can make the difference between long-term recovery and prolonged hardship. Financial resilience is about more than just weathering tough times—it's about adapting, planning, and building habits that foster long-term financial security and peace of mind. This chapter explores personal stories of recovery, practical strategies, and the importance of financial literacy in overcoming adversity.

Personal Stories of Financial Recovery

Real-life examples can offer valuable insights into how individuals have overcome significant financial setbacks, providing inspiration and practical lessons for others. Our experiences are replete with such stories.

Rebuilding After Bankruptcy

Susan, a single mother of two, faced the daunting reality of filing for bankruptcy after a failed business venture. Her financial situation spiraled out of control because of mounting debt, and she felt defeated. However, after attending financial counseling, Susan started from scratch by creating a detailed budget, cutting unnecessary expenses, and gradually building an emergency savings fund. It took her several years, but she successfully rebuilt her credit, returned to financial stability, and even launched a new, more sustainable business.

Bouncing Back from Job Loss

James had been working at a stable job for nearly 15 years when, without warning, his company downsized, leaving him unemployed. With a family to support and limited savings, James initially struggled with the fear of uncertainty. However, instead of panicking, he used the setback as an opportunity to gain new skills. He took online courses, networked extensively, and accepted freelance gigs while searching for a full-time position. Six months later, he landed a new job in a different industry with better pay and more flexibility.

Surviving a Medical Crisis

Angela and her husband were financially secure until a medical crisis left them with thousands of dollars in bills. They were unprepared for the extent of the expenses and fell into significant debt. Angela sought the help of a financial advisor, who worked with them to negotiate payment plans with medical providers and consolidate their debt. They also attended workshops on financial literacy, which helped them understand insurance policies better and plan for future medical emergencies.

These stories demonstrate that financial recovery is possible, even from dire circumstances. What unites these individuals is not just their perseverance but their willingness to adapt, learn, and seek support when needed.

Strategies for Financial Resilience

Building financial resilience involves more than just cutting back on expenses during tough times. It requires a proactive approach to managing finances and preparing for unexpected challenges. Here are some essential strategies:

Emergency Fund Creation

An emergency fund is a financial cushion designed to cover unforeseen expenses like medical emergencies, car repairs, or job loss. Experts recommend saving at least three to six months' worth of living expenses in a liquid, easily accessible account. This buffer can provide peace of mind and prevent financial hardship from spiraling out of control.

Budgeting and Expense Tracking

The first step toward financial resilience is understanding your income and expenses. One sure way to financial ruin is to live beyond your means. Creating a budget allows you to live within your means and allocate money toward savings. Tracking expenses, whether through apps or manually, helps you identify areas where you can cut costs or reallocate funds toward essential needs and long-term goals.

Diversifying Income Streams

Relying on a single source of income can leave individuals vulnerable to financial instability. Diversifying income streams, whether through side businesses, investments, or part-time work, helps create additional safety nets. This also provides more flexibility during times of uncertainty.

Debt Management

High levels of debt, especially with high interest rates, can quickly become unmanageable during financial crises. Prioritizing debt repayment, consolidating loans where possible, and negotiating lower interest rates are effective ways to regain control over finances. Additionally, developing a habit of minimizing unnecessary debt and avoiding reliance on credit cards for non-essential purchases can build long-term resilience.

Investing in Skills and Education

Investing in personal and professional development can increase financial resilience by making individuals more adaptable in the job market. Learning new skills, acquiring certifications, or exploring different industries can open doors to new opportunities, even in challenging economic conditions.

Reflection Prompt: Reflect on your current financial habits. How prepared are you for an unexpected financial challenge? What steps can you take today to improve your financial resilience? Consider creating or reviewing your budget, assessing your emergency fund, and researching options for diversifying your income.

Learning Financial Literacy Skills

Financial literacy—the ability to understand and apply financial concepts such as budgeting, investing, and managing debt—is a critical component of resilience. Without financial literacy, even those who are earning well can find themselves in precarious situations. Often, it is not how much you earn that matters, it is what you do with what you earn. Here are some key areas of financial literacy that everyone should prioritize:

Understanding Credit Scores

A credit score affects your ability to borrow money, secure housing, and even qualify for jobs. Learning how credit works—understanding the factors that contribute to credit scores and knowing how to improve or maintain a good score—can open doors and provide leverage in financial negotiations.

Basic Investment Knowledge

Investing wisely can generate additional income streams and grow your wealth over time. Many people avoid investing owing to a lack of knowledge or fear of risk, but basic financial education on topics like mutual funds, stocks, bonds, and retirement accounts can help build long-term wealth with manageable risk.

Debt Management Skills

Learning how to manage debt effectively is a cornerstone of financial health. This includes knowing how to prioritize debts, negotiate payment terms, and understand the long-term impact of interest rates and late fees.

Insurance and Risk Management

Understanding different types of insurance (health, home, life, auto) and how they fit into your overall financial plan is key to protecting yourself against future financial adversity. Being underinsured can lead to catastrophic costs while being overinsured can strain your finances unnecessarily.

Reflection Prompt: Consider your current level of financial literacy. Are there areas where you feel uncertain or uninformed? Commit to learning more about those topics, whether through books, courses, or financial counseling.

Conclusion

Financial resilience is about building a foundation that can withstand economic adversity, whether on a personal or global scale. By learning from others' stories of financial recovery, implementing practical strategies, and committing to improving financial literacy, anyone can improve his/her financial resilience. The key is to remain proactive, adaptable, and resourceful in both good times and bad. Developing these habits not only prepares you for financial challenges but can lead to greater financial freedom and stability over the long term.

Further Reading

James, Elijah M. *Wealth Creation and Preservation.* EJ Publishing, 2024.

Orman, Suze. *The Nine Steps to Financial Freedom: Practical and Spiritual Steps So You Can Stop Worrying.* Crown Business, 1997.

Ramsey, Dave. *The Total Money Makeover: A Proven Plan for Financial Fitness.* Thomas Nelson, 2003.

Robin, Vicki, and Joe Dominguez. *Your Money or Your Life: 9 Steps to Transforming Your Relationship with Money and Achieving Financial Independence.* Penguin Books, 2008.

Chapter 8
Mental Health Resilience

Introduction

Mental health resilience is the ability to adapt and thrive despite the emotional and psychological challenges that life may present. In a world where anxiety, depression, and stress are increasingly common, learning how to build mental health resilience is more important than ever. This chapter will explore real-life stories of individuals who have faced mental health challenges, offer strategies to build daily habits that foster emotional strength, and provide practical exercises for reflection.

Navigating Mental Health Challenges

Mental health challenges, such as depression, anxiety, and post-traumatic stress disorder (PTSD), affect millions of people worldwide. These conditions can be overwhelming, yet many individuals find ways to adapt and grow stronger through resilience. Below are a few stories that highlight the power of mental health resilience.

Sophia's Story: Overcoming Anxiety

Sophia was a high-achieving professional who struggled with anxiety after a series of setbacks in her career. Panic attacks began to interrupt her workday, and she felt unable to cope. Through therapy, mindfulness, and gradual exposure to anxiety-inducing situations, she was able to reclaim her life. Building resilience for Sophia involved confronting her fears step by step and embracing self-compassion.

James' Journey: Managing Depression

James experienced major depressive episodes after losing his job and going through a divorce. He felt isolated and hopeless. With the support of a mental health professional and through journaling and setting small, achievable goals, he slowly rebuilt his sense of purpose. His story is one of perseverance, emphasizing the role of external support and self-reflection in building resilience.

Maya's Battle with PTSD

After surviving a traumatic car accident, Maya struggled with post-traumatic stress disorder. Flashbacks, nightmares, and hypervigilance affected her daily life. Through cognitive-behavioural therapy (CBT) and connecting with a trauma support group, Maya found strategies to cope with her PTSD. Her journey illustrates that mental health resilience often requires structured support and understanding.

Building Daily Mental Health Habits

Resilience in mental health is not built overnight; it is a process that involves developing consistent habits to maintain emotional well-being. Here are some key practices to foster mental resilience:

Mindfulness and Meditation

Engaging in mindfulness exercises, even for a few minutes a day, can help reduce stress, improve focus, and bring greater emotional stability. Practices like deep breathing and progressive muscle relaxation are accessible ways to start.

Regular Physical Activity

Physical exercise is one of the most effective ways to boost mental health. It releases endorphins and helps reduce symptoms of depression and anxiety. Simple activities like walking, yoga, or light aerobics can be immensely beneficial for mental resilience.

Cognitive Reframing

Cognitive reframing involves changing the way you view a stressful situation. By consciously adjusting negative thoughts into more positive or neutral ones, individuals can reduce the emotional impact of stress. This technique is commonly used in CBT (cognitive-behaviour therapy)to foster mental toughness.

Social Connections

Building and maintaining strong social relationships is a key element of resilience. Staying connected with friends, family, or support groups provides emotional support, which is crucial during tough times.

Reflection Exercise: Identifying Personal Coping Mechanisms and Support Networks

In this reflection exercise, take time to think about how you currently handle stress and mental health challenges. Answer the following questions:

What are my current coping mechanisms for handling stress, anxiety, or other emotional struggles?

List out the strategies you use, whether it's talking to a friend, engaging in a hobby, or using specific relaxation techniques. Reflect on how effective these methods have been for you.

Who is part of my support network?

Consider the people in your life who offer support when you're feeling down. Identify friends, family members, colleagues, or professionals who help you cope. Acknowledge how often you reach out to them and how they contribute to your resilience.

What new habits can I incorporate into my daily life to strengthen my mental health?

Think of one or two small habits you can introduce into your routine, such as a five-minute mindfulness practice or a regular walk in nature. These small steps can make a big difference over time.

Conclusion

Building mental health resilience requires a blend of internal strength, external support, and consistent habits. It is an ongoing process that helps individuals cope with life's challenges with greater emotional fortitude. By learning from real-life stories, implementing daily practices for well-being, and reflecting on personal coping mechanisms, readers can take actionable steps to enhance their mental health resilience.

Further Reading

Neff, Kristin. *Self-Compassion: The Proven Power of Being Kind to Yourself.* HarperCollins, 2015.

Siegel, Daniel J. *The Mindful Brain: Reflection and Attunement in the Cultivation of Well-Being.* W.W. Norton & Company, 2007.

Part IV
Thriving Beyond Adversity

Chapter 9
Transforming Failure into Growth

Introduction

Failure is often seen as a setback, something to be avoided or feared. However, failure can also serve as one of life's most valuable teachers, providing insights and lessons that fuel personal growth. Many of history's most successful individuals have experienced significant failures before achieving greatness, using those moments as stepping stones to success. In this chapter, we'll explore how to reframe failure, learn from our mistakes, and transform these experiences into catalysts for growth.

I believe: *"You never fail until you stop trying."* This motivational saying has been attributed to Albert Einstein, Thomas Edison, and athlete Florence Griffith Joyner. I don't know with whom it originated, but I believe that many others have echoed the remark that carries a deep truth.

Stories of Personal Transformation

Throughout history, there have been countless stories of individuals who faced significant setbacks only to rise stronger. These narratives serve as powerful examples of resilience, demonstrating how failure can lead to personal and professional transformation when embraced with the right mindset.

J.K. Rowling:
From Rejection to Global Success

Before her *Harry Potter* series became a global phenomenon, J.K. Rowling faced numerous rejections from publishers. Struggling with financial difficulties as a single mother, she persisted, refining her manuscript despite repeated setbacks. Rowling's resilience in the face of rejection underscores the importance of perseverance. Her ability to use failure as motivation illustrates how personal setbacks can fuel future success when viewed as opportunities for learning.

Thomas Edison:
Failure as a Path to Innovation

Thomas Edison's invention of the lightbulb didn't happen overnight. He famously remarked, "I have not failed. I've just found 10,000 ways that won't work." Edison's story highlights how failure is an integral part of the innovation process. Each "failure" brought him closer to his eventual success. His experience teaches us that reframing failure as experimentation can lead to breakthrough achievements.

Sara Blakely: Embracing Failure Early

Sara Blakely, founder of Spanx, credits her father for instilling in her the value of failure. At the dinner table, he would regularly ask, "What did you fail at today?" This created a mindset where failure wasn't feared but embraced. Blakely's resilience allowed her to transform a simple idea into a billion-dollar company, showing how adopting a positive relationship with failure can lead to extraordinary results.

These stories remind us that failure is not the end of the road but an essential part of any success story. By embracing setbacks, we can cultivate the resilience needed to transform failure into a stepping stone for growth.

Learning from Mistakes

While failure can feel painful and discouraging, it is essential to view it as a learning experience. Here are some strategies for turning failure into growth:

Analyze the Situation Objectively

The first step in learning from failure is to analyze it without emotion. What went wrong? Was it a lack of preparation, misjudgment, or external factors? Taking the time to understand what led to the failure helps in identifying areas of improvement.

Own Your Mistakes

Accept responsibility for your role in the failure. Acknowledging mistakes rather than blaming others allows you to regain control of the situation. It demonstrates maturity and a willingness to grow, which are critical in developing resilience.

Extract Lessons from the Experience

Each failure contains valuable lessons. Reflect on what you learned from the situation. Did it expose a weakness that needs attention? Did it provide insights into a more effective approach? Write down key takeaways to ensure the lessons stick and inform your future decisions.

Implement Changes and Move Forward

After extracting lessons from failure, the next step is to implement necessary changes. This could mean adopting new strategies, refining your approach, or seeking guidance from mentors. Once the changes are in place, move forward without dwelling on the past. Resilience requires the ability to bounce back quickly after setbacks.

Reflection Example: Turning Personal Failure into Growth

In this exercise, reflect on a time when you experienced failure—whether in your career, relationships, or personal goals. Answer the following questions to help you process the experience and identify ways to grow from it:

What was the failure, and how did it impact you emotionally and mentally?

Describe the situation in detail, noting how it made you feel and what immediate effects it had on your life. Acknowledge the emotions tied to the experience without judgment.

What factors contributed to the failure?

Were there specific actions, decisions, or external circumstances that led to the failure? Break down the event into smaller components to understand what went wrong.

What key lessons can you take away from the experience?

Reflect on what you learned from the failure. Did it teach you to be more prepared? Did it highlight a skill that needs improvement or a mindset that needs adjusting?

What changes will you implement to prevent a similar failure in the future?

Outline specific steps you can take to ensure that the lessons from your failure are put into action. Focus on what you can control in future situations.

How can this experience make you more resilient moving forward?

Consider how the process of overcoming this failure has strengthened your ability to handle adversity in the future. How can you use this experience as motivation to face future challenges with confidence?

Conclusion

Failure is not the end of the road but a crucial part of the journey toward growth. By analyzing our failures, owning our mistakes, and extracting valuable lessons, we can transform setbacks into powerful opportunities for learning and development. The stories of personal transformation remind us that failure is a universal experience, but resilience allows us to rise above it. With the right mindset and tools, each failure can become a stepping stone to greater success.

Further Reading

Brown, Brené. *Daring Greatly: How the Courage to Be Vulnerable Transforms the Way We Live, Love, Parent, and Lead.* Avery, 2012.

McGonigal, Kelly. *The Upside of Stress: Why Stress Is Good for You, and How to Get Good at It.* Avery, 2016.

Sivers, Derek. *Anything You Want: 40 Lessons for a New Kind of Entrepreneur.* Portfolio, 2011.

Chapter 10
Building Resilience Through Faith and Spirituality

Introduction

Resilience is often seen as an inner strength that allows individuals to cope with hardships, but for many, faith and spirituality serve as crucial foundations for building this resilience. Spirituality provides a lens through which to view suffering, loss, and personal trials, offering hope and strength in times of darkness. Faith is not merely about religious belief; it's also about trusting in something greater than oneself, finding meaning in difficult experiences, and cultivating a sense of peace and purpose.

This chapter delves deeply into how faith and spirituality fuel resilience by sharing stories of individuals who have overcome significant adversity through their beliefs, exploring spiritual practices that foster inner strength, and offering practical exercises to deepen readers' spiritual resilience.

Stories of Spiritual Resilience

A Pastor's Journey Through Grief

Pastor John, a well-loved spiritual leader in his community, faced one of the most difficult moments of his life when he lost his wife to cancer. This was the man, who, for decades, was a tower of strength not only for members of his church but also for anyone who needed his help. One of his favourite sayings was, "Lean on Me." However, as he dealt with the overwhelming grief, he questioned his faith. Despite his doubts, he chose to lean on his community and the spiritual teachings he had shared with others. By praying daily, serving his congregation, and finding solace in scripture, Pastor John was able to heal. His journey inspired others in his church to find strength in their faith during their own challenges.

Mary's Journey Through Loss

Mary lost her only son in a tragic car accident, leaving her devastated and questioning her faith. For months, she felt lost and angry, unable to find solace. Over time, her faith community rallied around her, offering support, prayers, and companionship. Slowly, through daily prayers and meditating on God's promise of eternal life, Mary found peace in believing she would be reunited with her son in the afterlife. Her journey of spiritual resilience transformed her grief into a deepened faith, and today, she leads a grief support group for others who have lost loved ones.

Jack's Recovery from Addiction

Jack battled substance addiction for over a decade, during which time he lost his job, his home, and his relationships, including his wife and daughter. After hitting rock bottom, Jack entered a faith-based rehabilitation program that introduced him to the power of prayer, scripture, and a higher purpose. With the support of his faith community, Jack embraced a new way of life. Faith gave him the strength to fight his addiction, and today, Jack credits his spirituality for helping him stay sober and rebuild his life. His story of resilience demonstrates how faith can provide a foundation for personal recovery.

Shalini's Spiritual Transformation

Shalini was diagnosed with a chronic illness that confined her to a wheelchair. Feeling angry and betrayed by life, she struggled to accept her new reality. Over time, she began attending a meditation center where the teachings focused on inner peace and acceptance through mindfulness. Through daily meditation, Shalini found not only peace but also the strength to embrace her new identity. She now volunteers at the center, sharing her story of resilience with others, reminding them that spiritual resilience is not about changing circumstances, but about finding peace within them.

Spiritual Practices that Support Resilience

Prayer and Meditation

Prayer and meditation are powerful tools for building resilience, providing comfort during challenging times, and fostering a deeper connection to the divine. Prayer can offer solace, allowing individuals to share their fears and burdens with God, while meditation helps cultivate inner calm, emotional balance, and mindfulness in the present moment. Studies have shown that prayer and meditation reduce stress and anxiety, leading to better-coping mechanisms in the face of adversity.

Scripture Reading

Reading sacred texts offers individuals guidance and inspiration, providing examples of how faith leaders overcame adversity. Stories from the Bible, the Quran, or other religious texts highlight themes of perseverance, trust in God's plan, and finding meaning in suffering. Reflecting on these teachings can inspire resilience, showing that adversity is a part of life but can be overcome with faith.

Acts of Service

Many spiritual traditions emphasize the importance of serving others. Engaging in acts of service, whether through volunteering, helping a neighbour, or providing support within a faith community, strengthens resilience by fostering purpose and connection. Helping others during one's own difficult times can alleviate feelings of helplessness, reminding individuals of their capacity to make a difference.

Rituals and Ceremonies

Participating in spiritual rituals and ceremonies—such as attending religious services, lighting candles, or fasting—creates a structured way of reconnecting with one's faith. These rituals offer a sense of continuity, grounding individuals in their spiritual identity, especially during turbulent periods. They reinforce a connection to something greater than oneself, a reminder that resilience is often about leaning into one's faith when personal strength feels depleted.

Reflection Exercises

Spiritual Strength Journal: Take 10 minutes each evening to reflect on how your faith has helped you cope with challenges during the day. Write down three ways in which your spirituality provided comfort or strength. Reflect on specific moments where prayer, scripture, or support from your faith community strengthened your resolve.

Guided Prayer for Resilience: Set aside time for a guided prayer focused on building resilience. Begin by acknowledging your current challenges, then ask for divine guidance and strength to face these obstacles. End the prayer with words of gratitude for the strength you have already received.

Gratitude Meditation: Spend 5 minutes each morning in gratitude meditation. Focus on the blessings in your life, no matter how small, and connect them to your spiritual beliefs. Reflect on how these blessings foster resilience and provide hope during difficult times.

Faith-Based Community Service: Volunteer in your local community or faith-based organization. Serving others fosters a sense of purpose and connection, helping to strengthen your resilience while also uplifting those around you. After each service experience, reflect on how it has enhanced your personal spiritual growth.

The Interconnection of Mind, Body, and Spirit

True resilience is a holistic process that involves the mind, body, and spirit working in harmony. While faith and spirituality support the soul, it is equally important to nurture the mind through positive thinking and emotional strength, and the body through proper care and healthy practices. A spiritually resilient person recognizes that faith extends beyond belief—it also requires physical and mental resilience to endure life's hardships fully.

Spirituality often helps bridge the gap between the emotional and physical aspects of resilience. For instance, spiritual practices such as yoga and Tai Chi combine physical movement with mindfulness and spiritual reflection, building both physical and mental resilience. Similarly, meditation not only fosters spiritual connection but also improves mental clarity and emotional balance.

Conclusion

Building resilience through faith and spirituality is a deeply personal journey. For some, it may involve prayer, scripture, and religious community, while for others, it might be about connecting with a sense of purpose, mindfulness, or divine presence. As seen in the stories and practices shared throughout this chapter, spirituality can provide comfort, guidance, and hope, transforming adversity into an opportunity for growth. By cultivating spiritual resilience, individuals can not only endure life's difficulties but also find meaning and strength along the way.

Further Reading

James, Elijah M. *The Power of Prayer: A Christian Manifesto.* EJ Publishing, 2024.

Nouwen, Henri J.M. *The Inner Voice of Love: A Journey Through Anguish to Freedom.* Image Books, 1996.

Tutu, Desmond and **Mpho Tutu.** *The Book of Forgiving: The Fourfold Path for Healing Ourselves and Our World.* HarperOne, 2014.

Chapter 11
Using Creativity as a Resilience Tool

Introduction

Creativity is often thought of as a gift reserved for artists, writers, and musicians, but in truth, it is a powerful resilience tool accessible to everyone. When faced with adversity, engaging in creative expression can become a lifeline, offering an outlet for emotions, stress relief, and a way to process difficult experiences. This chapter explores how creativity can be used as a transformative tool to cultivate resilience, offering insight into creative expressions, how creativity fosters mental and emotional strength, and how to discover one's unique creative outlets.

Creative Expressions of Resilience

Throughout history, individuals have turned to creative practices as a means of overcoming life's challenges. From painting and writing to dance and music, creative expressions allow people to channel their inner struggles into something tangible, beautiful, and healing. Whether it is writing poetry about personal grief or painting abstract representations of difficult emotions, creativity helps externalize and process deep emotions that might otherwise be difficult to articulate.

For example, Frida Kahlo, the renowned Mexican painter, used her art to express the physical and emotional pain she endured after a severe accident and multiple health struggles. Similarly, Maya Angelou, a celebrated poet and writer, used her words to overcome and rise above personal trauma, inspiring others with her story of resilience. These examples show that creative expression can transform adversity into a powerful narrative of strength and hope.

Yo-Yo Ma's Journey

Yo-Yo Ma, one of the world's most famous cellists, has often spoken about how music served as a critical source of resilience throughout his life. Born to a family of musicians, Ma's journey with the cello began at a very young age. As he dealt with the pressures of an intense career in classical music, Ma found that playing music was not only a source of joy but also a form of therapy. During difficult times, especially when dealing with personal struggles, Ma turned to his instrument to ground himself. His passion for creative expression enabled him to process emotions in ways that words could not, and he has used his platform to advocate for the healing power of music.

During the COVID-19 pandemic, Ma shared his music virtually with the world to bring comfort to those experiencing isolation, fear, and grief. His #SongsOfComfort initiative, which began as an impromptu social media post of him playing Dvořák's *"Going Home,"* evolved into a global movement. For Ma, music became a way to build emotional resilience, not only for himself but also for millions around the world. His story highlights how creativity, in the form of music, can be a balm for the soul during times of crisis.

The Artistic Journey of Judith Scott

Judith Scott was born with Down syndrome and spent much of her early life in an institution, isolated from the world and misunderstood. When she was in her 40s, her sister Joyce gained custody of her and brought her to California, where Judith's life changed forever. Joyce enrolled her in Creative Growth Art Center, an art program designed for adults with disabilities. Though Judith did not initially seem interested in participating, she eventually discovered a profound connection with fiber art. She began wrapping found objects in layers of yarn, thread, and fabric, creating unique and intricate sculptures.

For Judith, art was more than just a creative outlet—it was her voice. Nonverbal throughout her life, she expressed her emotions, thoughts, and dreams through her sculptures, many of which grew into large, complex pieces. Her work gained recognition in the art world, and Judith Scott became an internationally acclaimed artist, with exhibitions in galleries and museums. Through her artistic process, Judith transformed her silence and isolation into a powerful, resilient form of expression. Her story is a testament to the profound role creativity can play in fostering resilience, particularly for those facing significant life challenges.

How Creativity Fosters Resilience

Creativity plays a unique role in fostering resilience because it allows for emotional expression and problem-solving in ways that traditional approaches might not. It engages different parts of the brain, promotes flexibility in thinking, and encourages seeing challenges from multiple perspectives. Research has shown that engaging in creative activities—such as writing, painting, or crafting—can reduce stress, boost mood, and even enhance the ability to cope with trauma.

When individuals create, they are given the opportunity to reflect on their experiences and emotions. This reflective process often brings clarity, helping them understand their challenges from a different viewpoint. For example, journaling can serve as an emotional release and help individuals track their personal growth over time. Similarly, creative movement, like dance, offers a way to release pent-up emotions physically.

A 2017 study published in the Journal *Art Therapy* found that even 45 minutes of creative activity significantly reduced cortisol levels (a stress-related hormone) in participants, showing that creativity has measurable psychological benefits.

By allowing individuals to externalize their emotions, creativity becomes a way to release tension and find peace amidst turmoil.

Finding Your Creative Outlet

One of the most rewarding aspects of using creativity as a resilience tool is that it is deeply personal. Not everyone resonates with traditional forms of art like painting or sculpture, but creativity can be found in various activities. Gardening, cooking, photography, or even creating vision boards can serve as creative outlets. The key is to find an activity that helps channel emotions and provides a sense of flow and accomplishment.

To help discover your creative outlet, consider the following steps:

Reflect on Your Interests

What activities make you feel alive or allow you to express yourself? These could be activities you enjoyed as a child or something you've always wanted to try.

Experiment with Different Forms

Try different forms of creative expression. Sign up for a pottery class, experiment with photography, or start journaling. Write a poem or a short story.

Let Go of Perfection

Creativity is not about producing perfect results. It's about the process of expression. Give yourself permission to create without judgment. You are not yet entering a competition, you are on a journey of discovery.

Incorporate It into Your Routine

Once you've identified your creative outlet, make it a regular part of your life. The more you engage in creative activities, the more resilience you'll build over time.

Reflection Exercise

Take a few moments to reflect on how creativity plays a role in your life. Consider these prompts:

What creative activities bring you joy or relief from stress? How do they help you process emotions or surmount challenges?

If you haven't explored your creative side, what new activity could you try? What steps can you take to begin incorporating creative expression into your routine?

Think of a time when you overcame a difficult situation. How might creativity have helped you during that time?

Conclusion

Using creativity as a resilience tool is about more than producing artwork or mastering a skill; it's about self-expression, problem-solving, and emotional healing. By embracing creative outlets, individuals can face their challenges with a renewed sense of strength and clarity. Whether through writing, painting, music, or other forms of creativity, these activities offer powerful ways to process difficult emotions and build the mental toughness needed to thrive in adversity. Creativity is not only a source of joy but also a key ingredient in a resilient life.

Further Reading

Kaufman, Scott Barry. *Wired to Create: Unraveling the Mysteries of the Creative Mind.* Perigee Books, 2016.

Leavy, Patricia. *Method Meets Art: Arts-Based Research Practice.* The Guilford Press, 2020.

Chapter 12
Lifelong Learning and Adaptability

Introduction

In today's rapidly evolving world, the ability to learn continuously and adapt to change has become more essential than ever. Lifelong learning—staying open to new experiences, acquiring new knowledge, and honing new skills throughout life—is no longer optional but a critical survival skill for many. Equally important is adaptability, the capacity to adjust to changing circumstances, environments, and challenges. Together, lifelong learning and adaptability help foster resilience, enabling individuals to manage uncertainty, overcome adversity, and thrive in both personal and professional settings.

This chapter will explore inspiring stories of resilient learners who have overcome significant challenges through their commitment to learning and adaptability. We will also discuss the role of curiosity in resilience, practical steps for cultivating a mindset of continuous learning, and reflection exercises to enhance adaptability. These stories and strategies demonstrate how lifelong learning can transform setbacks into opportunities for growth and success.

Stories of Resilient Learners

Nelson Mandela: Learning in Isolation

Nelson Mandela's resilience and commitment to learning during his 27 years of imprisonment are legendary. Despite harsh conditions, Mandela dedicated himself to education, studying law and history while organizing secret study groups for fellow prisoners. Mandela's ability to grow mentally while confined physically is a powerful reminder that learning can serve as both an intellectual pursuit and an act of defiance against oppression. His adaptability and commitment to growth, even in isolation, were key to his success in leading South Africa's peaceful transition from apartheid.

Malala Yousafzai: Defying Oppression Through Education

Malala Yousafzai is a symbol of resilience and advocacy for girls' education worldwide. After surviving a near-fatal attack by the Taliban, Malala continued her pursuit of education, eventually becoming the youngest-ever Nobel Prize laureate. Her belief in the transformative power of learning, even in the face of violence, highlights how education can build resilience. Malala's story demonstrates the courage to adapt to dire circumstances and turn tragedy into a global movement for change.

Richard Branson: A Relentless Entrepreneurial Spirit

Richard Branson, the founder of the Virgin Group, exemplifies resilience through adaptability and lifelong learning. Diagnosed with dyslexia, Branson struggled academically, yet he used this challenge to fuel his passion for entrepreneurship. Throughout his career, Branson faced numerous failures, from record label flops to failed ventures in the airline and space tourism industries. However, his ability to continuously learn from these failures and adapt his strategies made him one of the most successful and respected entrepreneurs in the world.

The Role of Curiosity and Adaptability in Resilience

Curiosity is the driving force behind lifelong learning. It encourages individuals to explore new areas, question existing assumptions, and remain open to fresh ideas and perspectives. Curiosity helps individuals see challenges as opportunities for growth rather than insurmountable obstacles. Those who are curious are more likely to embrace change, seek out new experiences, and pursue knowledge that fosters personal and professional development.

How to Increase Curiosity

Curiosity and resilience are closely connected. Curious people are resilient and resilient people are curious. If we increase curiosity, we increase resilience. According to the Resilience Institute, curiosity can be nurtured and developed with intentional practices. It suggests the following strategies to cultivate a curious mindset and enhance your resilience:

1. Ask Open-Ended Questions

The foundation of curiosity is inquiry. Develop the habit of asking open-ended questions—questions that don't have simple yes or no answers. For example, instead of asking, "Did you like it?" ask, "What did you find interesting about it?" Open-ended questions encourage deeper thinking and exploration, leading to richer conversations and greater understanding.

2. Embrace the Beginner's Mindset

The beginner's mindset is about approaching situations with the openness and wonder of a novice, even when you're experienced. This mindset allows you to see things from a fresh perspective, free from the assumptions and biases that can cloud judgment. To cultivate a beginner's mindset, try learning something new or engaging in activities outside your usual routine.

3. Follow Your Interests

Curiosity is fueled by passion. Identify the subjects, activities, or ideas that naturally intrigue you and pursue them with enthusiasm. Whether it's reading a book on a topic you're curious about, visiting a museum, or taking up a new hobby, following your interests keeps your mind engaged and fosters continuous learning.

4. Challenge Your Assumptions

We all have assumptions—preconceived notions about how the world works. Curiosity invites us to challenge these assumptions and explore alternative viewpoints. When faced with a decision or problem, ask yourself, "What if the opposite were true?" or "Is there another way to look at this?" This practice broadens your perspective and opens the door to new possibilities.

5. Cultivate Wonder

Wonder is a sense of awe and fascination with the world around us. It's a deep appreciation for the mysteries of life that sparks curiosity. To cultivate wonder, spend time in nature, observe the night sky, or immerse yourself in the arts. These experiences remind us of the vastness of the world and our small, yet significant, place within it.

6. Stay Open to Feedback

Curiosity thrives in an environment of openness and learning. Embrace feedback from others as an opportunity to grow and improve. Instead of viewing feedback as criticism, approach it with curiosity—what can you learn from it? How can it help you see things differently? This mindset not only enhances resilience but also fosters personal and professional development.

7. Engage in Lifelong Learning

Lifelong learning is a commitment to continuous growth and education. It's about being curious not just about specific subjects, but about life itself. Take courses, attend workshops, read widely, and seek out new experiences. Lifelong learning keeps your mind sharp, adaptable, and resilient in the face of change.

Source: https://resiliencei.com/blog/curiosity-the-catalyst-for-growth-and-resilience

Adaptability

Adaptability complements curiosity by allowing individuals to adjust to new environments, situations, or demands. In the workplace, adaptability means being open to learning new technologies, adjusting to changing job roles, or shifting strategies when faced with new challenges. In personal life, it may involve adjusting to major life changes, such as moving to a new city, starting a new career, or overcoming a personal setback. By combining curiosity with adaptability, individuals are better equipped to handle life's uncertainties and handle adversity with resilience.

Building a Lifelong Learning Mindset

The following steps will help you to build a lifelong learning mindset:

1. Stay Curious and Embrace New Challenges

One of the key ways to cultivate a lifelong learning mindset is by remaining curious and open to new challenges. Ask questions, seek out new knowledge, and embrace the unfamiliar. Whether it's reading a book on a new subject, taking a class, or learning a new hobby, staying intellectually curious helps build resilience by keeping your mind flexible and adaptable.

2. Reflect on Failures as Learning Opportunities

Failure is an inevitable part of life, but how we respond to it can make all the difference. Rather than viewing failures as setbacks, resilient learners see them as opportunities for growth. Ask yourself: What can I learn from this experience? What skills or knowledge can I gain to handle this situation better in the future? By shifting your mindset, you can transform failure into a powerful learning tool.

3. Engage in Continuous Learning

The world is constantly evolving, and staying stagnant is not a viable option. Make a firm commitment to engage in continuous learning, whether through formal education, online courses, mentorship, or self-directed study. The options are many. Lifelong learners remain open to new information and skills, staying adaptable to the changing demands of the world around them.

Reflection Exercise

Identifying Personal Growth Opportunities
Think of a recent challenge or setback you've experienced in your personal or professional life. Reflect on the following questions:

- What did this experience teach you?
- What skills or knowledge could you develop to better handle similar challenges in the future?
- How can you remain open to learning from both success and failure?

Write down your reflections and identify one area where you would like to grow. Set a specific goal for how you will pursue this growth, whether it's through taking a course, seeking mentorship, or reading about a new topic.

Exploring New Skills Identify a skill or subject you've always wanted to learn but haven't yet explored. Dedicate time each week to practicing or studying this new skill. As you progress, keep a journal of your experiences, noting any challenges you face and how overcoming them enhances your resilience.

Conclusion

Lifelong learning and adaptability are essential components of resilience. Whether navigating personal hardships, career setbacks, or global uncertainties, the ability to learn and adapt empowers individuals to overcome adversity and thrive. The stories of Nelson Mandela, Malala Yousafzai, J.K. Rowling, and Richard Branson illustrate how curiosity and adaptability can transform even the most daunting challenges into opportunities for growth. By fostering a mindset of continuous learning, we not only equip ourselves to face life's obstacles but also open ourselves to the endless possibilities of growth, success, and personal fulfillment.

Further Reading

Dweck, Carol S. *Mindset: The New Psychology of Success.* Random House, 2006.

Duckworth, Angela. *Grit: The Power of Passion and Perseverance.* Scribner, 2016.

Seligman, Martin E.P. *The Hope Circuit: A Psychologist's Journey from Helplessness to Optimism.* PublicAffairs, 2018.

Part V
Moving Forward with Resilience

Chapter 13
Building a Resilient Community

Introduction

Resilience is often considered an individual trait, but when faced with widespread challenges, such as natural disasters, economic downturns, or pandemics, communities must band together to overcome adversity. A resilient community is one that not only survives hardship but emerges stronger and more connected because of it. Such resilience is built on shared values, collaboration, and collective efforts to support one another.

The capacity for communities to demonstrate resilience often stems from their ability to create networks of support and communication. By sharing resources, knowledge, and emotional support, people within these communities can withstand significant disruptions and challenges. This chapter explores real-life stories of community resilience, strategies to build and sustain strong communities, and ways individuals can assess and enhance their own contributions to local and global communities.

The Importance of Community

Happiness.com identifies the following seven benefits of community.

1. Support and safety

Living with uncertainty has become the norm during the COVID pandemic. This has made it more important than ever to have a strong support network in place. Indeed, one of the main reasons behind the importance of community is that it can help fight feelings of hopelessness and give us the certainty that we are safe when surrounded by our community. Furthermore, the benefits go both ways, since supporting others also gives *us* a boost.

2. Connection and belonging

Togetherness is so central to our experience as humans; that feeling we are part of something bigger can help give meaning to our lives. Finding others with the same values, interests, and world views makes us realise that we're not alone and makes us feel valued. Indeed, belonging highlights why community is necessary: being accepted into a group gives us a stronger sense of self and can help us cope with negative experiences and feelings.

3. Influence

Sometimes we need an extra push to stop us from falling into unhealthy habits or thoughts.

Experiencing the positive influence of like-minded people is another reason behind the importance of community. Studies confirm that our overall health is partly determined by our ability to look after ourselves, but sometimes we simply don't feel capable of it. Communities can influence us and motivate us to invest in our well-being and to bring positive changes to our lives.

4. Sharing

Sharing activities, ideas and feelings reinforces not only our sense of self, but also adds worth and value to the community. Indeed, the more the merrier applies in this case! That's not to mention the huge beneficial effect sharing can have on mental health: higher engagement, positive emotions, and empowerment are only some of the benefits. Sharing is caring.

5. Learning

Communities are usually built around common interests, but that doesn't mean they're homogeneous. We can still find people within them who have different views, experiences, or beliefs, and learning from them can help us reach insights that we may not have reached on our own.

6. Acceptance

Developing community bonds with others who have different views may be challenging, but it's also an opportunity to practise acceptance. I had a personal breakthrough when I read this article and understood that acceptance doesn't necessarily imply agreement.

7. More connections, more chances of success

The importance of community goes beyond the personal sphere and extends to professional development. Since the pandemic begun we've seen a stronger focus on supporting local businesses, so this is a good place to start networking and building strong relationships. You never know where that could take your business idea or professional life.

https://www.happiness.com/magazine/relationships/the-importance-of-community/

Collective Resilience Stories: How Communities Come Together During Adversity

New Orleans Post-Hurricane Katrina

In 2005, Hurricane Katrina devastated the city of New Orleans, displacing hundreds of thousands of residents and causing massive infrastructure damage. In the aftermath, the resilience of the city's communities was put to the test. Neighbours banded together to help each other rebuild homes, share food, and care for the elderly and vulnerable. Local organizations played a crucial role in the recovery effort, offering everything from legal aid to mental health services. One standout example was the Common Ground Collective, a grassroots organization that emerged shortly after the hurricane to provide basic services like medical care, legal advocacy, and housing assistance to the hardest-hit areas.

While rebuilding took years, the communities that came together in the face of devastation showcased remarkable resilience. The spirit of cooperation and mutual aid during the recovery process illustrates how collective action, shared responsibility, and community solidarity can foster strength in the most challenging circumstances.

Global Response to COVID-19

The COVID-19 pandemic posed one of the greatest global challenges of recent times, forcing communities across the world to adapt to unprecedented health, economic, and social crises. While some governments struggled with responses, local communities rose to the occasion, organizing mutual aid groups, food drives, and online support networks. In Italy, for example, neighbours who were isolated by strict lockdown measures found creative ways to connect. Residents took to their balconies to sing songs, share messages of hope, and foster a sense of solidarity despite physical distance.

The pandemic demonstrated the importance of resilience at both local and global levels. Many individuals found ways to offer help, whether by delivering groceries to elderly neighbours or by donating to health workers. The lessons learned from the pandemic about adaptability, resourcefulness, and solidarity will be critical in facing future global crises.

Fukushima Nuclear Disaster Response

In 2011, the Tōhoku earthquake and tsunami caused a devastating nuclear disaster at the

Fukushima Daiichi power plant in Japan. Thousands of people were displaced, and entire towns were rendered uninhabitable. Despite these overwhelming challenges, communities across Japan responded with an extraordinary display of resilience. Volunteers from across the country organized to support evacuees by providing shelters, distributing food and supplies, and assisting with the rebuilding of communities.

Local farmers and fishermen, who lost their livelihoods, demonstrated remarkable adaptability by learning new skills, such as organic farming or starting small businesses. These efforts showcased how communities could transform tragedy into opportunity by working together and supporting one another.

Strategies for Community Building and Support: Volunteering, Organizing, and Leading

To cultivate a resilient community, individuals and organizations must actively work to build social bonds, foster trust, and create networks of support. Below are several strategies to strengthen communities and enhance resilience:

1. Volunteering and Civic Engagement

Volunteering is one of the most direct ways to build community resilience. By donating time, energy, and skills to support local causes, individuals can help bridge resource gaps and strengthen social connections. Volunteerism also fosters a sense of purpose, belonging, and pride within a community. Whether it's organizing food drives, tutoring children, or participating in neighbourhood cleanups, volunteer efforts make tangible contributions to community resilience.

2. Organizing and Leading Community Initiatives

Local leadership is crucial for guiding communities through crises. Leaders help coordinate efforts, allocate resources, and create spaces where individuals can voice concerns and collaborate. One effective method of organizing is creating neighbourhood associations or community groups that regularly meet to discuss issues and brainstorm solutions. These groups provide an opportunity for residents to get to know one another, share resources, and prepare for future challenges.

For instance, after natural disasters like hurricanes or floods, well-organized community groups often play a pivotal role in disseminating information, distributing relief supplies, and providing immediate assistance to affected families. Leadership within these groups is essential for maintaining momentum and ensuring that all community members, especially vulnerable populations, are supported.

3. Creating Social Networks of Support

Strong social networks are at the heart of resilient communities. These networks can take many forms: informal neighbourly relationships, formal support groups, or online communities. During times of crisis, such networks allow individuals to share resources (food, water, shelter), offer emotional support, and stay connected despite physical isolation.

One example of a community network in action is the concept of "time banks," where community members exchange services—like childcare, home repairs, or tutoring—without exchanging money. Instead, they bank "hours" that they can redeem for services in the future. These systems foster community cooperation and resource sharing, reinforcing resilience at a local level.

Reflection Exercise: Assessing and Strengthening Local and Global Connections

Building a resilient community requires introspection about the networks and connections we cultivate. The following reflection exercise encourages you to assess your current community involvement and consider ways to strengthen both local and global connections:

Reflection Questions:

1. How connected do you feel to your immediate community? Are you actively involved in any neighbourhood groups or initiatives?

2. Do you know your neighbours? How often do you communicate with them or offer mutual support?

3. Are there local causes or organizations that align with your values and interests? How

might you contribute to them, either through volunteering or leadership?

4. On a global level, how do you stay informed about issues affecting other communities around the world? Have you considered supporting international causes through donations or advocacy?

5. In times of crisis, how would you rely on your local and global networks for support? Conversely, how could you contribute to the well-being of others?

Action Steps:

Identify one local cause or community group to become involved in, either through volunteering or participation in discussions.

Strengthen relationships with your neighbours by initiating conversations, organizing a block party, or offering to help with a community event.

Consider how your professional skills or hobbies might contribute to the resilience of your community. Can you teach a class, offer free services, or mentor others?

Conclusion

A resilient community is not built overnight. It requires sustained effort, cooperation, and a willingness to support one another in times of both prosperity and hardship. The stories of New Orleans after Hurricane Katrina, global communities during the COVID-19 pandemic, and the response to the Fukushima disaster highlight the incredible strength that communities can exhibit when faced with adversity. By fostering volunteerism, organizing local initiatives, and building strong social networks, communities can enhance their ability to face future challenges with resilience.

As individuals, we have the power to contribute to community resilience by engaging in meaningful ways—whether through volunteering, leading initiatives, or simply offering support to those around us. In doing so, we build stronger, more connected communities that can withstand the inevitable ups and downs of life.

Further Reading

Aldrich, Daniel P. *Building Resilience: Social Capital in Post-Disaster Recovery.* University of Chicago Press, 2012.

Putnam, Robert D. *Bowling Alone: The Collapse and Revival of American Community.* Simon & Schuster, 2000.

Chapter 14
Sustaining Resilience Over the Long Term

Introduction

Resilience is not a one-time achievement; it's a lifelong practice. For resilience to be sustained over the long term, individuals must cultivate habits, mindsets, and behaviours that allow them to adapt to and thrive through challenges. This chapter explores how to maintain resilience as a continuous journey, drawing from real-life examples and practical strategies that can be integrated into daily life. We'll discuss how to transform setbacks into stepping stones and how the cumulative effect of resilience can lead to long-term growth and fulfillment.

Real-life Stories

Oprah Winfrey: Rising Above Early Hardships

Oprah Winfrey's story of resilience begins with her difficult upbringing. Born into poverty and facing abuse in her childhood, Winfrey did not allow these early adversities to define her future. Her path to success was not immediate—she encountered numerous professional and personal setbacks, including being fired from a job as a news anchor. However, she demonstrated incredible resilience, using her life experiences to build empathy and connection with others. Winfrey's journey shows how resilience, when sustained through challenges, can lead to profound personal and professional success.

Viktor Frankl: Finding Meaning in the Worst Circumstances

Holocaust survivor Viktor Frankl offers one of the most remarkable stories of sustained resilience. During his time in Nazi concentration camps, Frankl developed the belief that life has meaning, even in the most miserable conditions. His ability to maintain mental resilience allowed him to survive emotionally and physically. Frankl's philosophy, later encapsulated in his book *Man's Search for Meaning*, teaches that resilience is deeply tied to finding meaning in suffering and maintaining hope in the darkest times.

Helen Keller: Thriving in the Face of Disability

Born deaf and blind, Helen Keller overcame immense obstacles to become an author, educator, and activist. Her lifelong resilience is evident in how she transformed her physical limitations into an opportunity for advocacy, becoming a symbol of triumph over adversity. Keller's perseverance, combined with the support of her teacher, Anne Sullivan, shows the power of resilience as a tool for continuous growth and empowerment. Her story teaches us that with the right mindset and support system, even the greatest obstacles can be overcome.

Resilience as a Lifelong Journey

Resilience is not something that people build once and then rely on indefinitely. It is a continuous process that evolves as life presents new challenges and opportunities. Long-term resilience involves adapting strategies and approaches to meet the changing nature of adversity throughout one's life.

The Evolution of Resilience

As people grow older, their approach to resilience must also evolve. For example, individuals in their 20s might rely on optimism and physical energy to push through setbacks, whereas those in their 50s may draw on emotional intelligence and experience. Each stage of life brings new opportunities for learning, growth, and adaptation. Understanding that resilience is an evolving skill set helps individuals remain open to new ways of thinking and problem-solving.

Reflection as a Tool for Growth

Reflection is key to maintaining long-term resilience. By regularly evaluating how they have handled challenges, individuals can identify their strengths and areas for improvement. Reflecting on past experiences not only helps people learn from their mistakes but also provides a sense of accomplishment and confidence in their ability to handle future challenges.

Daily Practices for Maintaining Resilience

Sustaining resilience over time requires embedding certain habits into daily life. These practices help build a strong foundation for mental, emotional, and physical well-being.

Mindfulness and Meditation

Mindfulness is the practice of staying present in the moment and accepting it without judgment. Incorporating mindfulness or meditation into your daily routine helps reduce stress, increases emotional regulation, and allows individuals to approach challenges with clarity and calm. Studies have shown that regular mindfulness practice can change the brain in ways that enhance resilience.

Physical Health and Well-being

Maintaining physical health is crucial to resilience. Regular exercise, good nutrition, and adequate sleep strengthen the body and improve mental health, providing the energy and focus needed to cope with adversity. Physical activity, even something as simple as a daily walk, can significantly reduce feelings of anxiety and depression, which are often barriers to resilience.

Emotional Regulation Techniques

Learning how to manage one's emotions effectively during challenging times is a key element of resilience. Techniques such as deep breathing, journaling, or practicing gratitude help individuals stay balanced and avoid being overwhelmed by negative emotions. Emotional regulation enables people to respond to challenges with composure rather than react out of fear or anger.

The Power of Positive Relationships

Social connections are vital for sustaining resilience over the long term. Building and maintaining supportive relationships provides a network of people to turn to in times of difficulty. Friends, family, and community members offer emotional support, encouragement, and sometimes even practical solutions during challenging moments. Maintaining these relationships requires effort, but it is a key pillar in long-term resilience.

Lifelong Learning

As noted in a previous chapter, continual learning is a key component of resilience. The ability to adapt to new information, skills, and environments enhances one's ability to cope with challenges. Whether it's learning a new language, picking up a new hobby, or taking on a challenging project at work, the act of learning keeps the brain sharp and improves problem-solving abilities, both of which are essential to resilience.

Setting Goals for Continued Growth

Setting goals is an important aspect of sustaining resilience because it provides direction and motivation. Clear goals offer a sense of purpose and focus, helping individuals move forward even when faced with challenges.

Personal Growth Goals

Personal development goals could include improving emotional regulation, learning new coping strategies, or pursuing hobbies that bring joy and fulfillment. By continually striving to become better versions of themselves, individuals cultivate a mindset of resilience that prepares them for future challenges.

Professional Development Goals

Setting professional goals can help individuals stay engaged and motivated in their work, even in the face of setbacks. These goals might include furthering education, advancing in a career, or acquiring new skills. Maintaining a growth-oriented mindset in the workplace fosters resilience, as individuals learn to view challenges as opportunities for growth.

Resilience-focused Goals

Setting goals specifically aimed at enhancing resilience—such as maintaining a daily mindfulness practice, exercising regularly, or nurturing relationships—helps individuals build the mental, physical, and emotional strength needed for long-term resilience.

Conclusion

Resilience is not a static trait; it is a dynamic, lifelong process that evolves as individuals grow and face new challenges. Stories like those of Oprah Winfrey, Viktor Frankl, and Helen Keller highlight how resilience can be cultivated and sustained over the long term. Through daily practices that prioritize emotional regulation, mindfulness, physical well-being, and strong relationships, individuals can continue to build their resilience. Setting personal, professional, and resilience-focused goals keeps individuals moving forward and adapting to life's inevitable adversities. Ultimately, resilience is not just about bouncing back from setbacks—it is about thriving and growing stronger with each new challenge.

Further Reading

Brown, Brené. *Rising Strong: How the Ability to Reset Transforms the Way We Live, Love, Parent, and Lead.* Random House, 2015.

Frankl, Viktor. *Man's Search for Meaning.* Beacon Press, 1959.

Neff, Kristin. *Self-Compassion: The Proven Power of Being Kind to Yourself.* HarperCollins, 2011.

Conclusion: Reflecting on Your Resilience Journey

Summarizing Key Takeaways

As we conclude this exploration of resilience, it's essential to reflect on the many lessons and tools that have been shared throughout the book. At its core, resilience is the ability to adapt and recover from adversity, but it is also much more than that—it's about growth, learning, and transforming challenges into opportunities for personal and collective empowerment.

We've seen that resilience isn't a fixed trait but a dynamic process that can be cultivated over time. Whether through mental health strategies, financial recovery, or spiritual growth, resilience is a skill that can be strengthened by daily practices, reflection, and conscious effort. Several key tools have been emphasized:

Embracing failure as a learning opportunity

Failure is not the opposite of success, but a stepping stone toward growth. Throughout the book, we've explored stories of individuals who have turned setbacks into breakthroughs, reminding us that mistakes are often our greatest teachers.

Community and support systems

One of the most powerful ways to build resilience is by nurturing strong relationships and support networks. Whether in personal, professional, or community contexts, relying on others—and offering support in return—is a vital part of staying resilient.

Daily habits and reflection

Building resilience is a long-term commitment. Simple daily practices like mindfulness, journaling, exercising, and expressing gratitude all serve to reinforce a mindset of adaptability and strength. Reflecting on how we handle adversity also helps us grow stronger with each new challenge.

Looking Forward with Hope and Determination

Resilience is not only about coping with past and present challenges, but also about preparing for future ones. As life continues to present new difficulties—whether they are personal, professional, or global—our capacity for resilience equips us to face them with hope and determination.

Looking ahead, the resilience strategies shared in this book can serve as a foundation for approaching the future with a sense of purpose. Whether you are dealing with ongoing financial difficulties, coping with mental health issues, or fostering resilience in relationships, the lessons learned here can provide guidance for staying grounded and motivated.

As we have seen in the stories of resilient individuals, growth is often the result of struggle. Each challenge faced builds character, strength, and wisdom. By committing to resilience, you are choosing to grow through whatever the future holds, transforming adversity into an opportunity for self-improvement and success.

Encouraging Personal Reflection

To conclude, I encourage you to reflect on your own resilience journey. Take time to consider the challenges you've overcome, the support systems you've relied on, and the personal growth you've experienced. Reflection is a powerful tool in understanding your strengths and identifying areas where you can continue to build resilience.

Here are a few final reflection prompts to reinforce your personal resilience:

- What past challenges have helped shape your character today?

- Who are the people in your life who provide support during tough times, and how can you strengthen those connections?
- What daily practices or habits can you integrate into your life to reinforce resilience?
- How can you turn future challenges into opportunities for growth and learning?

Resilience is a journey, not a destination. As you move forward in life, continue to apply the tools and lessons shared in this book to remain strong in the face of adversity, and to inspire resilience in those around you. Remember, each challenge is an opportunity to grow, and every setback is a chance to rise stronger than before.

By reflecting on the concepts presented, you can ensure that resilience becomes a lifelong practice, shaping how you approach adversity and triumph alike.

www.ingramcontent.com/pod-product-compliance
Lightning Source LLC
Chambersburg PA
CBHW051549010526
44118CB00022B/2639